# A DORLING KINDERSLEY BOOK
Conceived, edited, and designed by DK Direct Limited

## Note to parents

**What's Inside? Cars** is designed to help young children understand how cars work, from an ordinary family car to a pollution-free, solar-powered car. It shows how to st and start a vintage car, how the inside of a stretch limo lives up to its luxury image, and where to hide top-secret papers in a jeep. It is a book for you and your child to read and talk about together, and to enjoy.

**Editor** Hilary Hockman
**Designer** John Strange
**Typographic Designer** Nigel Coath
**U.S. Editor** Laaren Brown

**Illustrators** Ron Ballard, Ray Hutchins/Linden Artists,
Icon Design, Barry Robson/Linden Artists, Pete Serjeant
**Photographers** Ralph Hall, Andy Willshire
**Written by** Alexandra Parsons
**Consultant** John Farndon
**Design Director** Ed Day
**Editorial Director** Jonathan Reed

**Picture Credits** Batricar Ltd. (p. 10), G.M. Hughes Electronics Corp. (pp. 16–17)
Special thanks to the Police Department of the City of New York

First American Edition, 1993
10 9 8 7 6 5 4 3 2 1

Published in the United States by
Dorling Kindersley, Inc., 232 Madison Avenue
New York, New York 10016

Library of Congress Cataloging-in-Publication Data
Cars. – 1st American ed.
    p.  cm. – (What's inside?)
    Summary: Describes the functions and inner workings of
various vehicles, including a family car, jeep, and luxury limousine.
    ISBN 1-56458-219-1
    1. Automobiles – Juvenile literature. [1. Automobiles.]
I. Dorling Kindersley, Inc.  II. Series.
TL147.C339  1993
629.222 — dc20                         92–54272  CIP  AC
Printed in Italy

# WHAT'S INSIDE?

# CARS

DORLING KINDERSLEY
LONDON • NEW YORK • STUTTGART

# VINTAGE CAR

This 1903 De Dion Bouton looks like an open cart with a comfy leather sofa perched on top. That's because early, or vintage, cars like this were based on carriages drawn by horses. At first, cars were called "horseless carriages." Cars have changed a lot since then, but the basic parts are still the same.

This is the steering wheel. It turns the front wheels left or right.

There was no accelerator pedal. The driver controlled the speed by moving this lever backward or forward. Top speed was 25 miles an hour.

Here's the all-important handbrake!

When the driver put on the brakes, leather bands around a drum at the center of each of the back wheels squeezed the drums and stopped the wheels from turning.

The rod that joins a pair of wheels together is known as an axle.

The axle is attached to a spring.

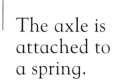

Coaches had panels at the front called dashboards to keep the driver from getting "dashed" by stones thrown up by the horses' hooves. In today's cars, the instrument panel is still called the dashboard.

Beep, beep! This is the horn. Early cars were difficult to stop, so it was important to warn people to keep out of the way.

Beautiful brass oil lamps gave out a soft yellow light.

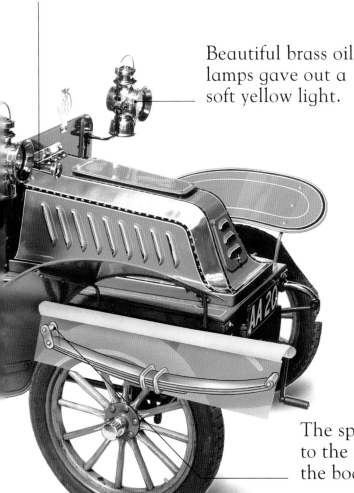

Starting a car in 1903 was really hard work. The driver turned this handle to get the engine parts moving. Then he had to leap into the driver's seat to operate the gears and the accelerator lever.

The springs are joined to the underside of the body, or chassis.

# FAMILY CAR

Look under the hood of most modern cars and you'll find
the engine. The engine works by burning gasoline inside small
chambers called cylinders. As the gas burns, it swells up
very quickly and pushes drums called pistons up and down.
The fumes from the burned gas come out through
the exhaust pipe at the back of the car.

The battery provides the electricity
to get the spark plugs sparking,
the headlights beaming, and the
tape player working.

The distributor
sends the spark to
the right cylinder.

This is the spark plug that makes
the spark to set the gas alight.

Gasoline is mixed with air in these
cylinders. It burns when the tiny
spark sets the mixture afire.

These pistons are
pushed up and down by
the burning mixture.

The crankshaft changes the up-
and-down movement of the pistons
into a round-and-round movement.
This makes the flywheel spin.

The spinning flywheel turns gears
rods that make the wheels go roun
Off we go – and don't forget the n

Engines need oil to keep
all the moving parts moving
smoothly. Oil goes in here.

# RACE CAR

Here's a car you can't drive to the mall! It's not even allowed on the road. Specially designed for race tracks, this Williams Formula One can do 210 miles an hour.

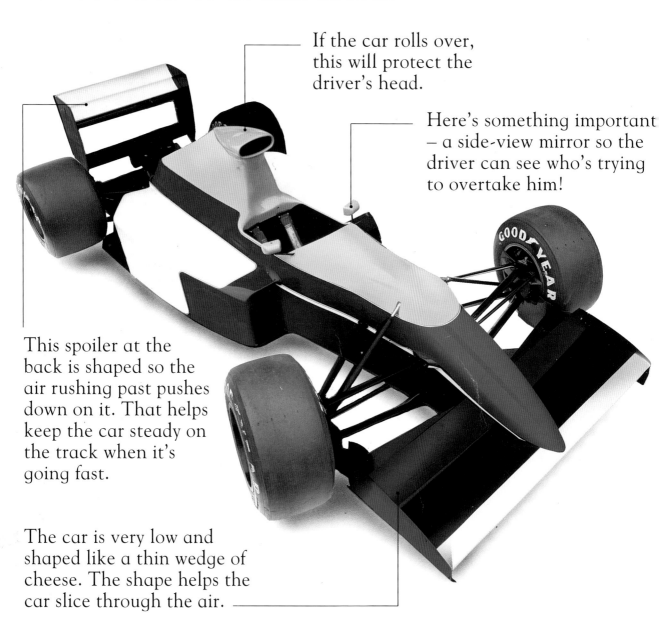

If the car rolls over, this will protect the driver's head.

Here's something important – a side-view mirror so the driver can see who's trying to overtake him!

This spoiler at the back is shaped so the air rushing past pushes down on it. That helps keep the car steady on the track when it's going fast.

The car is very low and shaped like a thin wedge of cheese. The shape helps the car slice through the air.

In the pit, a well-trained racing crew of 14 people can change all four wheels and have the car back in the race in eight seconds.

There's not much room inside! The seat is specially molded to fit the body of the driver of this car.

Racing tires are smooth and wide to grip the track on dry days. During a race, the tires get hot and start to melt. The sticky rubber helps keep the car on the track.

The engine sits between the back wheels.

These side pods are full of computers that check on the performance of the car and send the information back to the team in the pit.

On wet days they change to tires with treads.

# STRETCH LIMO

Wow! This is something special! A luxury limousine that's longer than most trucks. If you've got loads of money and want to show off in style, this is the car for you – an eight-wheeled Lincoln Town Car, built in 1989. Inside you'll find just about everything you'll need for your journey ... and more!

To make the stretch limo, a Lincoln was cut in half, and a new center section was fitted between the driver's seat and the back wheels.

With mirrored windows everywhere, you can check that you're looking good!

There's room inside for 15 passengers.

Here's the first-class compartment, where you can lounge on squashy pink suede sofas.

Only the front wheels are driven by the engine, so if they get stranded above the road, the back wheels can't move. Then it's time to get out and push!

Feeling thirsty? Here's the bar, with all kinds of drinks.

Want to get squeaky clean? Use one of the two whirlpool tubs in the back.

Forgotten anything? A toaster, food blender, hair dryer and a curling iron are stowed in a cupboard.

Tired? The seats turn into beds.

Bored? There are four television sets.

Want some music? There's a powerful stereo system with 44 speakers and disco lighting.

Want to phone home? Don't worry about a thing. Here's one of the four telephones.

# ELECTRIC CAR

Electric cars are quiet, and because they don't use gasoline they don't pollute the air. The trouble is, you can't go very far or very fast in an electric car like this one. It is designed to help people who have trouble walking. It can potter along the pavement at about four miles an hour, or it can travel on roads at twice that speed.

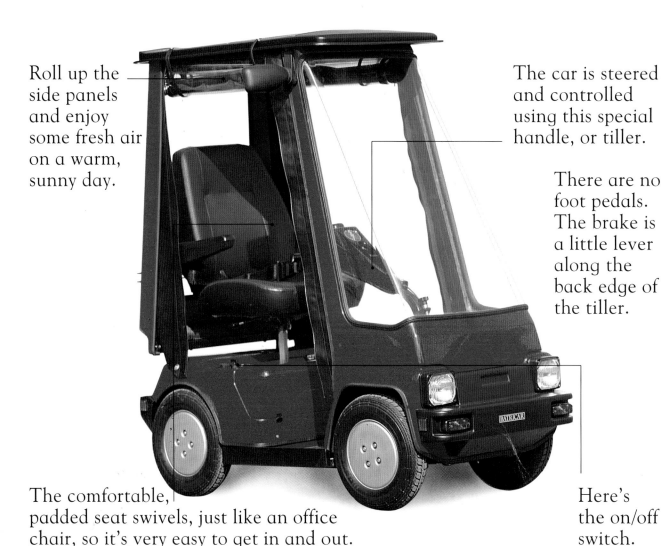

Roll up the side panels and enjoy some fresh air on a warm, sunny day.

The car is steered and controlled using this special handle, or tiller.

There are no foot pedals. The brake is a little lever along the back edge of the tiller.

The comfortable, padded seat swivels, just like an office chair, so it's very easy to get in and out.

Here's the on/off switch.

Here's another use for the electric car – out and about on the golf course.

A lever on the tiller controls your speed.

The motor turns a gear wheel, which turns a chain, which turns another gear wheel, which turns the back wheels. The motor is tucked away under the seat.

The batteries provide the power to make the motor work. The headlights run off the batteries, too.

When the batteries run low, they have to be recharged to give them a boost of power. That's why you can't travel far in this car.

BATRICAR

# POLICE CAR

This American police car has lots of jobs to do. It has to hurry to accidents, chase speeding cars, and sometimes take dangerous people to the police station. The police officers who drive around in it have to be able to keep in touch with headquarters.

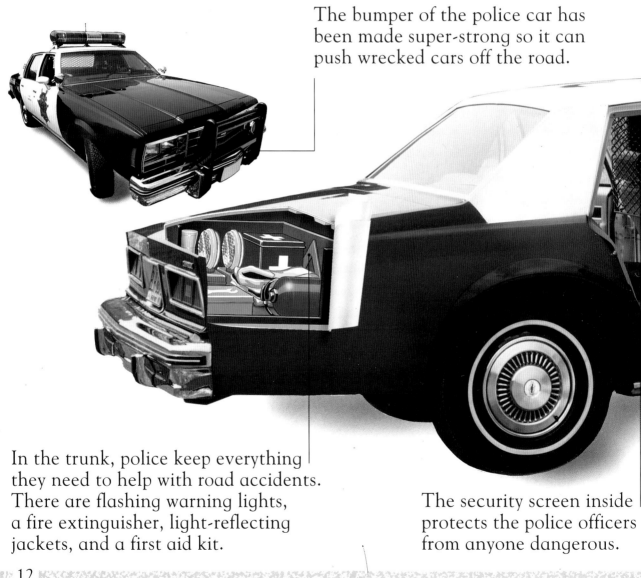

The bumper of the police car has been made super-strong so it can push wrecked cars off the road.

In the trunk, police keep everything they need to help with road accidents. There are flashing warning lights, a fire extinguisher, light-reflecting jackets, and a first aid kit.

The security screen inside protects the police officers from anyone dangerous.

In the Arabian desert, the police give chase on camels!

Here's the radio antenna that picks up the radio signals from the police station.

The flashing lights and sirens are attached to a bar that clips onto the roof like a roof rack.

Slow down! The radar gun can tell if other cars are breaking the speed limit.

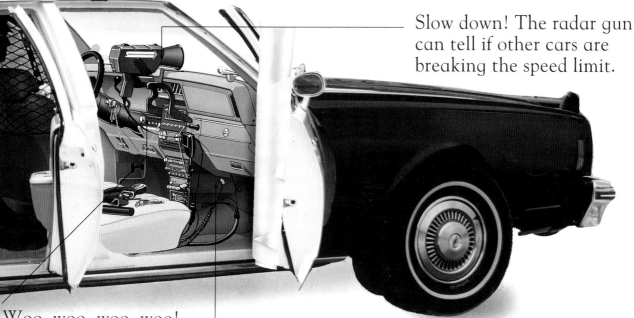

Woo, woo, woo, woo! These buttons operate the wailing sirens.

Here's the two-way radio. Officers can send messages to, and receive messages from, the police station on it.

# JEEP

This jeep is a 1943 U.S. Army Willys Phantom MB. It had to be strong and sturdy enough to tow heavy guns and carry vital supplies over fields and up and down hills. All four wheels are turned by the engine, so a jeep can bounce along over rough ground without getting bogged down or stuck in the mud.

The windshield folds down flat, so if the driver is under fire he won't be sprayed with broken glass.

The passenger seats can be folded down or even removed completely. With the seats out, the jeep can be loaded with supplies instead of people.

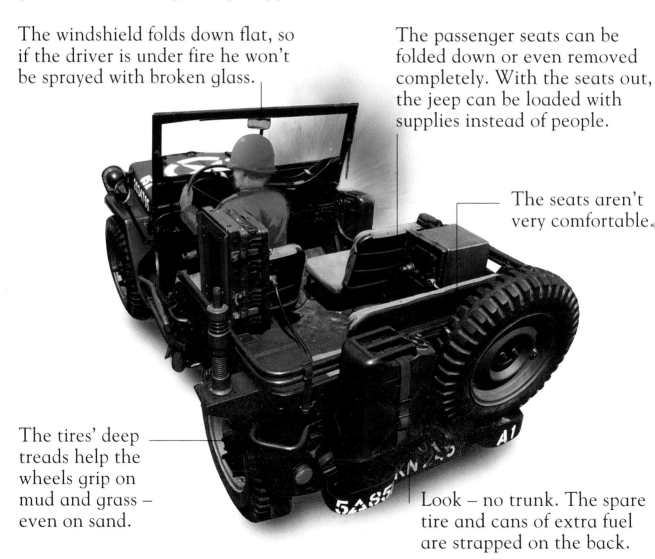

The seats aren't very comfortable.

The tires' deep treads help the wheels grip on mud and grass – even on sand.

Look – no trunk. The spare tire and cans of extra fuel are strapped on the back.

Spot the jeep! This jeep is painted in desert camouflage so it can't be seen by the enemy against the sand.

Sssh! Don't tell anyone! Top-secret papers can be kept in a zippered pocket in the seat cushion under the driver.

Jeeps have four-wheel drive – the front *and* back wheels are turned by rods coming from the engine.

Water from the radiator flows around the engine in a special casing called a water jacket. The water cools the engine.

The three gear levers make it possible to drive the jeep over desert sands or Arctic snow.

When the jeep hits a bump, this spring bends, then bounces back to its normal shape. That helps absorb the shock.

# SOLAR-POWERED CAR

This car needs no gas. It runs on energy from the sun, collected in a solar panel and stored in a battery. One day we may all be driving round in silent, pollution-free cars like this beautiful one-seater General Motors *Sunraycer*. It won a solar car race in sunny Australia in 1987, where it reached a record solar car speed of 35.22 miles an hour.

Here's the seat. It's like a mesh hammock, so air can flow through and around it to cool the driver.

The battery is charged with electricity from the solar panel.

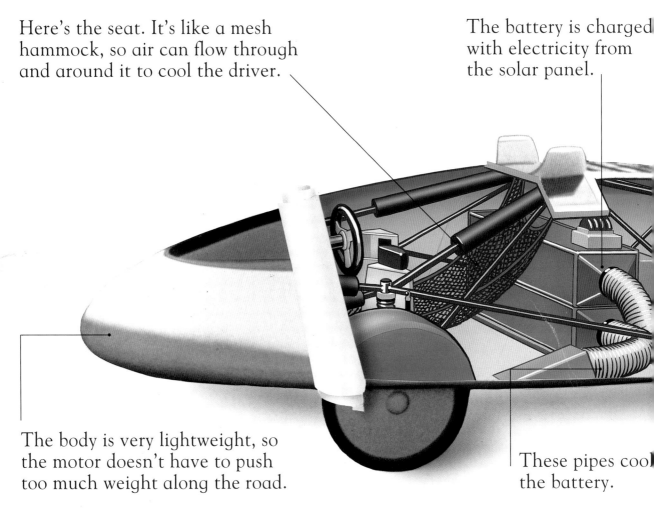

The body is very lightweight, so the motor doesn't have to push too much weight along the road.

These pipes cool the battery.

If your house is heated by solar panels, don't worry that the heat will go off if the sun isn't shining. Water heated by your solar panels can be stored and will keep heating your home, even at night.

Driving a solar car in the blazing sun can get very hot, so the canopy is made of special plastic to keep the driver cool. Its gold plating keeps out the sun's rays, but lets light in.

This is the solar panel. It looks like squares of black glass.

The solar panel is covered with 8,000 solar cells. They gather energy from the sun and turn it into electrical power. Each cell is the size of a small matchbox and the thickness of a piece of cardboard.

The special lightweight motor gets its power from the electricity stored in the battery.

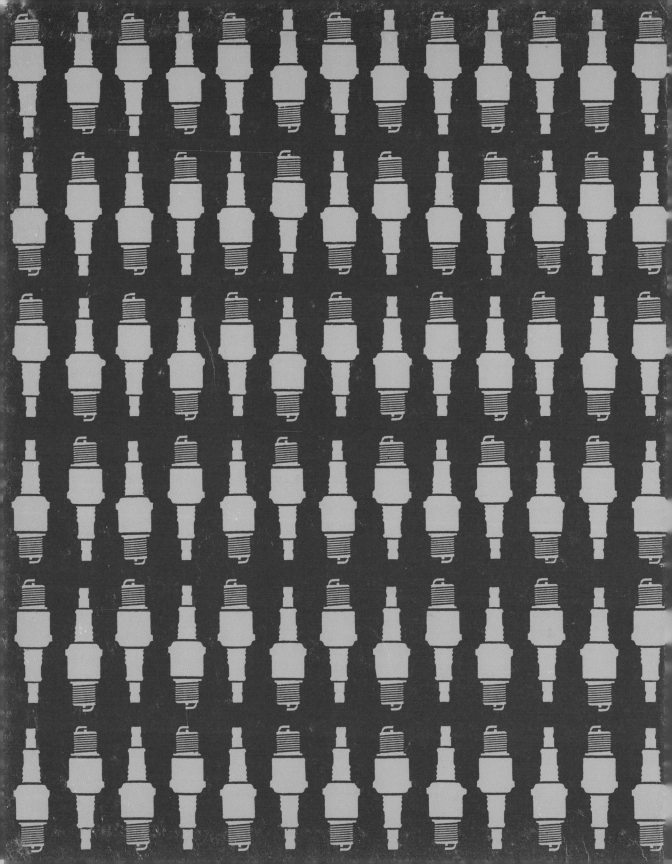